Kingdom
DIMENSIONS

Being Triumphant
Over all our Insecurities...

APMI Publications
a division of Kingdom Dimension Books
P.O. Box 17,
55051 Barga (LU),
Tuscany, Italy

We must turn our lives around,
by the renewing of our minds…

Upside down Kingdom

Dr. Alan Pateman

Kingdom DIMENSIONS

**Being Triumphant
Over all our Insecurities…**

BOOK TITLE:
Kingdom Dimensions–Being Triumphant over all our Insecurities

This edition published in 2025

Published by APMI Publications
A Division of Kingdom Dimension Books, Library No. **82**
P.O. Box 17,
55051 Barga (LU),
Italy

Email: publications@alanpatemanworldmissions.com
www.AlanPatemanWorldMissions.com

**APMI Publications and Kingdom Dimension Books are a division of
Alan Pateman World Missions**

Printed in the United States of America, Europe and Asia

Paperback ISBN: 978-1-918102-03-1
eBook ISBN: 978-1-918102-04-8

Acknowledgements:
Author/Design/Senior Editor/Publisher: Apostle Dr. Alan Pateman
Editing/Proofreading/Research: Dr. Jennifer Pateman
Computer Administration/Office Manager: Dr. Dorothea Struhlik
Cover Image Credit: www.PosterMyWall.com

*Where scriptures appear with special emphasis (**in bold,** italic or <u>underlined</u>) we have edited them ourselves in order to bring focused attention within the context of this subject being taught.*

*"God doesn't wait for Perfection,
He responds to Surrender."*

❖

Table of Contents

> Rewriting the Narrative of our Lives
> Chosen, Called, Secure *(Anchored in His Promises)*
> A Word on Rejection & Self Hatred *(Distorted Reflections)*
> Trusting the Rock, Not the Sand

> Competing vs. Completing His Will
> Hidden Rivalries and Homes That Hurt
> Security in the Finished Work

A Life of Forgiveness
The Secure Heart Forgives

Self-Centredness *(The Mirror That Lies)*
Narcissism & The Culture of Extreme Self-Love
Idolatry *(Self-Aggrandisement, Self-Adoration & Self-Worship)*
A Generation Blind to Its Own Exploitation *(Hyper-Sexual)*
The Small World of the Insecure Heart
When Church Becomes About Me
Marriage & The Mirror of Self
When Religion Reinforces Self
The Path to Healing

When Words Wound & The Tongue Divides
Death by a Thousand Opinions
Criticism vs. Compassion *(Jesus always Clothed Truth in Love)*
A Heart Quick to Fault *(Grace Given is Grace Returned)*
The Difference between Wounds that Heal & Ones that Scar
What Transformation Looks Like

A Heart That Can't Be Taught
Pride in Disguise
The Blind Spot of the Self-Righteous
Humility is the Posture of the Secure
A Teachable Spirit Changes Everything

❖

Cover Design Explained

I wanted to briefly explain the cover design — and the meaning behind it. What looks like an inverted world is, to me, a symbol of what I call *the upside-down Kingdom*.

Years ago, I read a book by Donald B. Kraybill titled *The Upside-Down Kingdom*. It deeply impacted me. It opened my eyes to how the Kingdom of God works — how it flips many of our assumptions on their head.

What we often see as "normal" in this world — sickness, brokenness, striving, pride — is not normal in the Kingdom. In fact, much of what we accept as natural is the opposite of God's truth.

God's ways are not our ways. His Kingdom runs counter to the culture around us. It challenges our emotions, our thinking, and our worldview. That's why Scripture calls us to *be transformed by the renewing of our minds.*

To walk in Kingdom reality, we must learn a new way of seeing, thinking, and speaking. It's not just a different message — it's a different world altogether.

THE INVERTED KINGDOM

At the heart of Jesus' life and teaching is one central theme: the Kingdom of God — what Matthew calls the Kingdom of Heaven.

This wasn't just a spiritual slogan. It was the defining message that set Jesus apart. Throughout the synoptic Gospels, the Kingdom is the thread that weaves through every parable, miracle, and proclamation.

Remove that thread, and the fabric of His message falls apart. It's not just part of what He taught — it is what He taught. But here's the shock: the Kingdom doesn't confirm our assumptions — it confronts them. It turns power structures, values, and expectations upside down. Or rather, it turns them *right-side up.*

RIGHT-SIDE-UP

If Jesus came to establish the Kingdom of God, maybe we've been naming it wrong. It's not upside down — it's *right-side-up.* It restores what life was always meant to be.

The Kingdom doesn't distort reality — it reveals it. What feels strange or backward is actually heaven putting things back in order. The image still works because it exposes how deeply we've normalised what's broken.

It also reminds us that society isn't level. We speak of "horizontal" relationships as if everyone stands on equal ground — but real life has peaks and valleys. Power, privilege, and access are not equally shared. The Kingdom sees all of it — and speaks into all of it.

CULTURAL NORMS & OSMOSIS

The phrase *upside-down* reminds us that God sees and challenges imbalance. His Kingdom doesn't ignore status — it often reverses it. It forces us to ask, *Why?* Why do we accept certain norms, values, and systems without question? From a young age, we absorb what's considered normal — success, beauty, power — not by reason, but by repetition.

Culture teaches us through exposure, not instruction. This subtle shaping — what we might call *social osmosis* — forms our worldview without us even noticing. But the Kingdom interrupts that autopilot. It wakes us up.

"Do not conform to the pattern of this world, but be transformed by the renewing of your mind" (Romans 12:2 NIV). Jesus calls us to see differently. Kingdom life means we don't accept things just because "that's how it is." We ask, *Is this how it should be — in light of who He is?*

FULL OF SURPRISES

The Kingdom of God is full of surprises. Again and again, through parables and interactions, Jesus upends expectations. The honoured are humbled, the outsiders welcomed, the disqualified forgiven. The ones we thought were in are left out.

His ministry is filled with paradox: the first become last, the poor are blessed, children are elevated, and sinners receive mercy — while the self-righteous are exposed. It's not how we think the world should work.

But that's the point. The Kingdom challenges everything we've accepted as normal. It overturns our definitions of success, power, and worth. And in that disruption, we begin to see clearly.

Some claim Jesus' teachings no longer fit our world. But the Kingdom He proclaimed speaks to every age — because it speaks to the heart. Pride, fear, injustice, and power games are as present now as ever.

The gospel doesn't lose relevance in a modern world — it reveals itself more fully. *"Heaven and earth will pass away, but my words will never pass away" (Matthew 24:35 NIV).*

The Kingdom is not just a future hope or a past moment — it is here, now. *"The Kingdom of God has come near to you." (Luke 10:9 NIV) "The Kingdom of God has come upon you" (Luke 11:20 NIV).* And Jesus' words still carry fire — burning through every excuse we make for the way things are.

Dr Alan

❖

Dedication

I lovingly dedicate this book, as always, to my dear and beautiful wife Jen, who really helps me and who is the intercessor behind this ministry, and has been so faithful over all of these years. I love her to bits. She is special. Also, to all my wonderful children — six of them! — and my 12 grandchildren *(and counting — because number 13 is on its way as we speak),* not excluding my first great-grandchild.

Yes, I know — God has blessed me richly and I am grateful beyond words — Psalm 127:3-5; 128:3,6; Pro 18:22. To name them all and honour them individually here, would take another book to complete! But they are all chosen and gifted. Destined for greatness.

God has something special for each one of you and you take up special residence in my heart. I love you all.

Husband, Dad and Grandad

❖

Acknowledgement

I want to thank everyone who's part of the team here at Alan Pateman World Missions *(CFE, LICU, and APMI Publications included).* Your contributions to this work, both seen and unseen, mean more than you know.

I'm also grateful to every pastor who ever pulled me aside after a service — yes, it happened more than once! — to gently, and lovingly, correct something they felt I may have expressed with more zeal than clarity in my younger years. At the time, it was a challenge. But those moments dealt with my personal pride, and they helped shape how I've ministered over the years. I honour you for that. *(God certainly builds the man before the ministry!)*

And finally, to one who helps keep things running behind the scenes — Dr. Dorothea. You manage the office with excellence and grace. What a wonderful job you do. We appreciate you more than words can say.

❖

Foreword

Welcome to a Journey Toward True Security
The Kind the World can't Give & Nothing can Take Away

It's a privilege to write the foreword for this book, "Kingdom Dimensions—Being Triumphant over all our Insecurities," because this is a message the world needs now more than ever.

Insecurity isn't a niche struggle—it's a human one. Whether masked by pride or exposed in fear, it affects how we see God, others, and ourselves. Older generations were taught to "toughen up," to survive. Today's younger generation? Crushed by emotion, comparison, and the craving to be seen. The expressions may differ, but the root remains the same: insecurity, and it's robbing us of joy, peace, and purpose.

But here's the hope: **God doesn't wait for perfection—He responds to surrender.** His love restores what insecurity breaks. In His presence is fullness of joy *(Psalm 16:11)*, and in His truth we become whole.

My husband Alan's words in this book carry timeless wisdom, drawn from Scripture and seasoned with grace. It's not self-help—it's soul help, eternal help. My prayer is that through these pages, you'll find the courage to lay down insecurity and rise into the identity God always intended for you: chosen, anchored, secure.

And whether you bought this book for yourself or someone else, you'll be glad you did!

Welcome to the journey.

Jennifer Pateman, Ph.D.,
Vice President of "Alan Pateman World Missions"
Co-Founder of "Connecting for Excellence International" and
"LifeStyle International Christian University,
author of *Millennial Myopia*

❖

Preface

For those who Long to Grow…

This is an inspiring and timely message for every believer who longs to grow into spiritual maturity. It's for those who, though children of God and fellow heirs with Christ *(Romans 8:17)*, feel trapped in a circular lifestyle—unable to move forward into the fullness God has prepared for them. This book was born out of a recent time of ministry to a precious group of people. In that moment, the Lord began to reveal deep truths, and a passionate desire was sparked within me: to see people break free from the mire of personal insecurities and step into the overflowing life of the Spirit *(Ezekiel 47:3-5, 12)*.

They confess Christ and believe in His finished work on the cross, yet they haven't embraced what lies beyond it. Kingdom living is on the other side of the cross. There is resurrection life *(Philippians 3:10)*, the baptism of the Holy Spirit *(Acts 1:8)*, and the power to reign in this life through Christ Jesus *(Romans 5:17)*. And yet many remain entangled in old mindsets, nursing insecurities, and speaking their fears rather than the promises of God.

God is calling us into our future. He desires that we live from a Kingdom perspective — even if we're not fully there yet. As Romans 12:2 *(NIV)* declares: "Do not conform to the pattern of this world, but be transformed by the renewing of your mind."

We are not meant to live by the limitations of a fallen nature, but according to our new birth rights *(John 1:12–13)*. Our spirits are saved, but our souls are being sanctified — transformed as we speak life, truth, and healing over ourselves through the Word of God *(Ephesians 5:26)*.

The trauma of insecurity is real and widespread. I know this personally. I've struggled with it deeply — especially when I was first called to preach. My insecurities were not surface-level; they were deeply rooted and often masked by other symptoms — pride, shyness, criticism, overindulgence, or avoidance. The problem with insecurity is that it rarely presents itself clearly. We deal with its effects without recognising its source. We try to fix the fruit, rather than address the root. This book is about confronting that root.

BITTER WATERS TURN SWEET

By spending much time in the Word of God, we can conquer the symptoms. But how much more effective would we be if we could see clearly the cause? When God heals the fountain, the bitter waters turn sweet *(2 Kings 2:21)*. This honest discussion is meant to offer biblical remedies for emotional immaturity, helping readers—young and old alike—move toward healing.

> Then Elisha went to the spring of water and threw the salt in it and said, "Thus says the LORD: 'I [not the salt] have purified and healed these waters; there shall no longer be death or barrenness because of it.'" So the waters have been purified to this day, in accordance with the word spoken by Elisha.
>
> 2 Kings 2:21-22 AMP

You'll find here practical wisdom, scriptural insights, and prayer that has helped me and others walk in victory. We will address topics like *insecurity vs. security, competition, criticism, inability to trust, narcissism, self-indulgence, and the difficulty many have with receiving correction.*

Let me be clear: we cannot walk as disciples of Christ with a spiritual limp. We cannot remain dull or indecisive. We are called to be salt and light *(Matthew 5:13–14)*, ambassadors of Christ *(2 Corinthians 5:20)*, and reflections of His glory *(2 Corinthians 3:18)*. Our lives must reflect the wholeness of Christ.

THE FULLNESS OF KINGDOM LIFE

This book offers help not just for individuals, but also for pastors, parents, teens, and those in leadership. It will provide tools for better counselling, healthier families, and stronger churches. I pray that what began as part of my own healing will now become part of yours—and that, together, we will walk in the fullness of Kingdom life.

As 2 Timothy 1:7 *(NIV)* reminds us: "For the Spirit God gave us does not make us timid, but gives us power, love and self-discipline." May that Spirit lead us into all truth, and may His healing transform every area of our lives — spirit, soul, and body *(1 Thessalonians 5:23)*.

Amen.

❖

Introduction

Born from Experience...

This book is a brief study on a very important subject, born from years of experience working with Christian believers from all walks of life. What I've discovered over time is that a significant number of people in the Body of Christ silently suffer from deep-rooted insecurity. Sometimes it's their own; other times it's the insecurity of those around them. Either way, it creates barriers to relationship—to growth, and to intimacy with God.

We are exploring real issues—spiritual, emotional, and relational struggles that touch many of us: insecurity, rejection, self-rejection, comparison, criticism, unforgiveness, and the inability to trust or take correction. These may not always be visible on the surface, but they operate like hidden viruses, affecting the way we think, feel, and live. It may surprise you that even in ministry and church life—among leaders and workers alike—these issues are alive and active. And if left unaddressed, they can hinder the very calling God has placed on our lives.

Yet Scripture offers us a powerful, eternal truth in Ephesians 1:3–4 *(NIV)*:

> Praise be to the God and Father of our Lord Jesus Christ, who has blessed us in the heavenly realms with every spiritual blessing in Christ. For He chose us in Him before the creation of the world to be holy and blameless in His sight.

This truth must become the foundation for how we see ourselves. We are not defined by what we've been through or what others have said about us. We are defined by the God who chose us before time began—not by accident, but with intentional, redeeming love. Despite this, many believers live as though their identity is still being negotiated by the culture around them. Bombarded daily by the noise of social media, public opinion, and worldly expectations, we slowly absorb lies about who we are—lies that say we're not enough, not worthy, or not lovable.

NEW IDENTITY

But we are Kingdom people, born again into a new identity. Romans 12:2 *(NIV)* urges us: "Do not conform to the pattern of this world, but be transformed by the renewing of your mind." Or as other translations say:

> And do not be conformed to this world [any longer with its superficial values and customs], but be transformed and

progressively changed [as you mature spiritually] by the renewing of your mind [focusing on godly values and ethical attitudes], so that you may prove [for yourselves] what the will of God is, that which is good and acceptable and perfect [in His plan and purpose for you].

Romans 12:2 AMP

Stop imitating the ideals and opinions of the culture around you, but be inwardly transformed by the Holy Spirit through a total reformation of how you think. This will empower you to discern God's will as you live a beautiful life, satisfying and perfect in his eyes.

Romans 12:2 TPT

Don't become so well-adjusted to your culture that you fit into it without even thinking. Instead, fix your attention on God. You'll be changed from the inside out. Readily recognise what he wants from you, and quickly respond to it. Unlike the culture around you, always dragging you down to its level of immaturity, God brings the best out of you, develops well-formed maturity in you.

Romans 12:1 MSG

This transformation is vital. We must renew our minds with the Word of God and allow the Holy Spirit to restore the places in us that have been wounded or misaligned. In fact, 2 Timothy 1:7 (NIV) says: "For the Spirit God gave us does not make us timid, but gives us power, love and self-discipline."

And yet, as I've traveled and ministered across nations and denominations, I have consistently seen this spirit of insecurity operating in the Church—quietly but effectively. Many don't even realise they're insecure. They assume it's just part of their personality: being shy, withdrawn, avoidant. But underneath, there's often a deep ache—a wounded place that hasn't yet encountered the healing truth of God's Word.

MY PERSONAL JOURNEY OF OVERCOMING INSECURITY

I've faced it too. In fact, when God first called me to preach, in my late twenties, I was overwhelmed by fear and self-doubt. I felt unworthy, unqualified, and deeply unsure of myself.

This journey led me to confront several other strongholds: comparison, the fear of man, self-centredness, and the inability to receive correction. Many of these stem from the carnal mind—the part of us that thinks like the world rather than with the mind of Christ. Proverbs 23:7 says, *"As a man thinks in his heart, so is he."* Transformation only comes when revelation hits the heart. And when it does, we become different—not only in theory, but in our thinking, our behaviour, and our relationships.

GENERATIONAL HONOUR & THE DANGER OF MISSED DISCIPLESHIP

There's a growing idea that older leaders need to honour the youth more. But true honour flows both ways—and it begins with a heart to serve.

> **He will turn the hearts of the fathers to their children, and the hearts of the children to their fathers** [a reconciliation produced by repentance], so that I will not come and strike the land with a curse [of complete destruction].
>
> Malachi 4:6 AMP

We're not called to father everyone. Our mission is to reach, teach, and walk *(work)* with the next generation in truth and love. But if younger believers aren't taught to serve others first—to walk in humility, not entitlement—we'll end up raising gifted people with no character.

And when that happens? We don't produce leaders—we create monsters. Leaders who dominate instead of disciple. People who divide rather than unify. A body that's insecure, unstable, and self-serving.

God's design is one body, many parts—all serving together. Every generation has a role. But the Kingdom isn't built through applause or ambition—it's built through honour, humility, and helping *(serving)* one another.

So, for the abundance of clarity, this isn't just a personal matter. The next generation—the future leaders of the Church—are watching us. Unfortunately, we are raising young people in a world that teaches *narcissism over servanthood, entitlement over humility.* And there's a reversal of honour, where older generations are expected to serve and honour the younger, instead of the biblical pattern of sons honouring fathers. This distortion will only feed further insecurity and rebellion unless we confront it with truth.

Again, this book does not aim to parent everyone—but it does call for responsibility. It calls us back to biblical discipleship, where leaders serve in humility, and believers learn to walk in identity. Ephesians 4:11–12 reminds us that Christ gave apostles, prophets, evangelists, pastors, and teachers to equip the saints for works of service—not so they could be celebrated, but so the Body of Christ would be mature, stable, and fruitful.

THE HOLY SPIRIT IS RAISING UP A SECURE, STRONG & SURRENDERED PEOPLE

We are in a critical hour. The days of "general's war" are shifting. This is "army war." Every believer is called. Every believer must be discipled. We are being equipped for the work of ministry, and that means we must become emotionally and spiritually whole. Insecurity cannot be our foundation.

The Holy Spirit is doing a work of healing in this generation—raising up a secure, strong, and surrendered people. But we must let Him begin with us. We must take ownership of our journey and decide: no more hiding, no more coping, no more shrinking back.

As Paul wrote in 1 Corinthians 13:11 *(KJV)*: "When I was a child, I spake as a child, I understood as a child, I thought as a child: but when I became a man, I put away childish things."

> When I was a child, I talked like a child, I thought like a child, I reasoned like a child; when I became a man, I did away with childish things. For now [in this time of imperfection] we see in a mirror dimly [a blurred reflection, a riddle, an enigma], but then [when the time of perfection comes we will see reality] face to face. Now I know in part [just in fragments], but then I will know fully, just as I have been fully known [by God].
>
> 1 Corinthians 13:11-12 AMP

Jesus Christ, our Lord, is the epitome of a secure person. Though fully God, He walked this earth fully man, depending on His Father for everything. That same Jesus now lives within us, and His security can become ours.

So I invite you — let's walk this road together. Let's heal, let's grow, and let's embrace the identity that is already ours in Christ. You are not who the world says you are. You are who God says you are.

Let the journey begin.

❖

CHAPTER 1

Security vs. Insecurity

Breaking the Cycle...

Every adult carries echoes of the child they once were. Deep within us live unresolved hurts, unmet needs, and unanswered questions— residues of childhood experiences that continue to shape our behaviours, attitudes, and relationships. These early wounds—whether from rejection, overindulgence, or a lack of affirmation—create unseen scars that linger well into adulthood.

REWRITING THE NARRATIVE OF OUR LIVES

Therefore if anyone is in Christ [that is, grafted in, joined to Him by faith in Him as Saviour], he is a new creature [reborn and renewed by the Holy Spirit]; the old things [the previous moral and spiritual condition] have passed away. Behold, new things have come [because spiritual awakening brings a new life].

2 Corinthians 5:17 AMP

If the voice of your younger self still whispers in your decisions or reactions, you're not alone. Many of the struggles believers face today—emotional outbursts, silent grudges, fear of failure—aren't just personality traits; they're evidence of unresolved insecurities. But the good news is this: Jesus doesn't just heal the symptoms—He transforms the root. He makes all things new *(2 Corinthians 5:17 NIV)*.

We must allow the love of our Heavenly Father to reach those hidden places. True healing requires honesty, and growth demands surrender. We're invited to trade our fears for faith, our weakness for His strength, and our insecurity for Kingdom identity. "For the mindset of the flesh is death, but the mindset controlled by the Spirit finds life and peace" *(Romans 8:6 TPT)*.

CHOSEN, CALLED, SECURE
(ANCHORED IN HIS PROMISES)

Too often, we try to fix the fruit without addressing the root. But transformation doesn't happen by ignoring the past— it comes by confronting it with the truth of God's Word. "Confess your faults one to another and pray one for another, that ye may be healed" *(James 5:16 KJV)*. Healing begins with acknowledgement.

Many adults today still react like children—pouting in silence, erupting in anger, clinging to grudges, or striving to prove their worth. Grown men fight to save face, marriages

34

break under emotional immaturity, and churches divide under spiritual insecurity. As someone wisely said, "You either parent the child within — or give in to him."

If salvation made us instantly perfect, there would be no church splits, no marital strife, no unresolved conflict. But clearly, we are all still growing. "We all... are being transfigured into His very image as we move from one brighter level of glory to another" *(2 Corinthians 3:18 TPT).* This transformation is a process — and that process is intentional.

God sees us through the lens of Christ's sacrifice. From the moment we're saved, we are declared righteous, holy, and complete *(Colossians 2:10).* But spiritual maturity requires more than a position — it demands progress. It means crucifying the flesh *(Galatians 5:24),* renewing our minds daily *(Romans 12:2),* and walking in newness of life *(Romans 6:4 NIV).*

A WORD ON REJECTION & SELF HATRED
(DISTORTED REFLECTIONS)

Insecurity doesn't always shout — it often whispers in self-destructive ways. What we believe about ourselves shapes how we treat our bodies, our minds, and even our future. Deep insecurity often masquerades as control, perfectionism, or detachment. It hides behind filters, diets, obsessions, and silence.

For some, it becomes orthorexia or anorexia, driven by the belief that thinner means better — or that controlling food can somehow control the chaos within. Others fall into cycles of bulimia, punishing themselves in secret for the shame they can't shake. These aren't simply medical disorders. Often, they're *manifestations of a deeper ache* — a longing to feel worthy, wanted, enough.

Then there's bullying — and more subtly, cyberbullying. Words thrown like daggers behind screens pierce just as deeply. Many who bully do so from their own insecurity, projecting pain onto others. But many more suffer silently under the weight of cruel words, comparisons, and rejection. "The tongue has the power of life and death..." — Proverbs 18:21 *(NIV)*

Whether the shame is shouted from others or whispered within, it distorts our self-perception. Insecurity causes us to look in the mirror and see flaws instead of fingerprints — mistakes instead of God's masterpiece. But here's the truth: "You are altogether beautiful, my darling; there is no flaw in you" — Song of Songs 4:7 *(NIV)*. "Don't you realise that your body is the sacred temple of the Holy Spirit...? You don't belong to yourself" — 1 Corinthians 6:19 *(TPT)*.

We were never meant to punish ourselves into perfection. We were made to walk in wholeness, not torment. God sees our struggles — and still calls us beloved! We must let Him reframe how we see ourselves. And gently uncover the wound beneath the behaviour. Our worth is not in how we look, what we weigh, or what others say. It's in Whose we are.

TRUSTING THE ROCK, NOT THE SAND

We don't earn God's approval through good works. Jesus fulfilled every law and bore every burden. "He became sin who knew no sin, so that in Him we might become the righteousness of God" *(2 Corinthians 5:21 NIV)*. Salvation is by grace through faith *(Ephesians 2:8–9)*, and all we must do is believe and receive Him as Lord and Saviour *(Romans 10:9–10 KJV)*.

So what's our role? We get to partner with Christ—to walk as co-heirs in His Kingdom *(Romans 8:17)*, to bear fruit that lasts *(John 15:16)*, and to reflect His glory to a watching world. We pray, we give, we love, and for these things we will one day hear, "Well done, thou good and faithful servant" *(Matthew 25:21 KJV)*.

Yet even powerful truths—like faith declarations, submission, or spiritual gifts—can become false securities if they replace our dependence on Jesus. When we rely more on methods than the Master, we misplace our hope. "For the Lord will be your confidence, firm and strong, and will keep your foot from being caught [in a trap]" *(Proverbs 3:26 AMP)*. Christ alone is our firm foundation *(1 Corinthians 3:11 KJV)*.

So let's not mistake performance for transformation. Let's not allow knowledge to substitute for intimacy. God is after the heart. And it's only when we allow Him to heal the deepest parts of us that true spiritual security can be formed.

PRAYER

Gracious Heavenly Father, more than anything, I long for Your character, Your love, and Your power to be seen in me. I want to reflect Christ in every thought, word, and deed. I surrender every fear, every insecurity, every false identity

I've carried. Shine Your light into every hidden place in my heart. I declare that I am a new creation in Christ *(2 Corinthians 5:17).* The old is gone—buried with Him. I no longer live under the shadow of who I once was but in the light of who I am in You.

> So from now on we regard no one from a human point of view [according to worldly standards and values]. Though we have known Christ from a human point of view, now we no longer know Him in this way.
>
> Therefore if anyone is in Christ [that is, grafted in, joined to Him by faith in Him as Saviour], he is a new creature [reborn and renewed by the Holy Spirit]; the old things [the previous moral and spiritual condition] have passed away. Behold, new things have come [because spiritual awakening brings a new life].
>
> But all these things are from God, who reconciled us to Himself through Christ [making us acceptable to Him] and gave us the ministry of reconciliation [so that by our example we might bring others to Him].
>
> 2 Corinthians 5:16-18 AMP

Let Your peace surround me. Let Your Word anchor me. Let Your Spirit guide me. I confess my faults before You, not in shame—but in faith. For You are faithful and just to forgive and to cleanse me *(1 John 1:9).* Today I choose freedom. I choose truth over fear, maturity over insecurity, and wholeness over wounds. Be glorified in me in Jesus' name. Amen.

❖

CHAPTER 2

Striving & Rivalry

Labouring in the Spirit, not the Flesh...

In a world that thrives on performance, competition often parades as ambition, strength, and drive. But beneath that drive, insecurity can quietly take root— especially when our worth is tied to achievement. From our earliest years, many of us were conditioned to compare and compete: for approval, for attention, for love. Whether on the playground, in the classroom, or later in our professions and ministries, the unspoken message remains: *You are only as valuable as your last success!*

COMPETING VS. COMPLETING HIS WILL

But God's Word paints a very different picture. In Christ, our value is not measured by wins or performance, but by the price He paid and the love He freely gave *(Ephesians 1:6*

KJV). We are already accepted – already seated with Him in heavenly places *(Ephesians 2:6 NIV).*

The Bible encourages us to pursue excellence: "Whatever you do, work at it with all your heart, as working for the Lord, not for human masters" *(Colossians 3:23 NIV).* But when our striving is driven by comparison instead of calling, excellence is corrupted by ego. That's when competition turns toxic. "For where envy and selfish ambition exist, there will be disorder and every evil practice" *(James 3:16 AMP).*

> But God, being [so very] rich in mercy, because of His great and wonderful love with which He loved us, even when we were [spiritually] dead and separated from Him because of our sins, He made us [spiritually] alive together with Christ (for by His grace—His undeserved favour and mercy—you have been saved from God's judgment).
>
> And He raised us up together with Him [when we believed], and seated us with Him in the heavenly places, [because we are] in Christ Jesus, [and He did this] so that in the ages to come He might [clearly] show the immeasurable and unsurpassed riches of His grace in [His] kindness toward us in Christ Jesus [by providing for our redemption].
>
> For it is by grace [God's remarkable compassion and favour drawing you to Christ] that you have been saved [actually delivered from judgment and given eternal life] through faith. And this [salvation] is not of yourselves [not through your own effort], but it is the [undeserved, gracious] gift of God; not as a result of [your] works [nor your attempts to keep the Law], so that no one will [be able to] boast or take credit in any way [for his salvation].

For we are His workmanship [His own master work, a work of art], created in Christ Jesus [reborn from above—spiritually transformed, renewed, ready to be used] for good works, which God prepared [for us] beforehand [taking paths which He set], so that we would walk in them [living the good life which He prearranged and made ready for us].

Ephesians 2:4-10 AMP

Jesus Himself confronted this in His disciples. When they argued over who was the greatest, He didn't rebuke their desire for significance—but He redefined it. "The greatest among you will be your servant" (Matthew 23:11 NIV). True greatness is never found in outshining others, but in laying your life down for them.

HIDDEN RIVALRIES AND HOMES THAT HURT

Even in church life, the spirit of competition can sneak in—disguised as excellence or zeal. Ministry teams become performance platforms. Fellowship becomes rivalry. Some churches recruit members not for discipleship, but for their talents—just to win the next sports league or worship showcase. But "Unless the Lord builds the house, the builders labor in vain" (Psalm 127:1 NIV).

Insecure leadership fosters insecure communities. When we compare ministries, giftings, or influence, we reveal hearts that haven't fully rested in God's design. "You are complete in Him" (Colossians 2:10 KJV). That means we have nothing to prove and no one to outperform. The measure of success is obedience to His call, not outperforming someone else's.

And what about at home? Sadly, many children grow up watching their parents play games of one-upmanship. Spouses interrupt and correct each other to appear more knowledgeable. Parents criticise each other in front of their children. In these moments, we model rivalry, not respect. Our homes become arenas instead of sanctuaries.

But it doesn't have to be this way. A secure home teaches that love isn't lost in losing, and value isn't gained in winning. Children should know that even when they fall short, they are still deeply loved — by their family and by God.

Jesus, the perfect Son of God, "made Himself nothing… taking on the nature of a servant" *(Philippians 2:7 NIV)*. He didn't grasp for status — He gave Himself away. And in doing so, He secured victory for all of us. "Thanks be to God, who gives us the victory through our Lord Jesus Christ" *(1 Corinthians 15:57 KJV)*.

SECURITY IN THE FINISHED WORK

Our goal isn't to crush competition, but to root out the insecurity that fuels it. When we're grounded in Christ, we can genuinely cheer for others, celebrate their strengths, and even lose without losing ourselves. "In all these things, we are more than conquerors through Him who loved us" *(NIV)*.

> Yet in all these things we are more than conquerors and gain an overwhelming victory through Him who loved us [so much that He died for us]. For I am convinced [and continue to be convinced—beyond any doubt] that neither death, nor life, nor angels, nor principalities, nor things present and threatening, nor things to come, nor powers, nor height, nor depth, nor

any other created thing, will be able to separate us from the [unlimited] love of God, which is in Christ Jesus our Lord.

Romans 8:37-39 AMP

As believers, we don't compete to earn identity — we live from the identity already secured for us. "You didn't choose me, but I chose you. I commissioned you to go out and bear fruit that will last" *(John 15:16 TPT)*. That's our call — not to outperform, but to out-serve. Not to compare, but to complete His will for our lives.

Let us raise families that honour rather than compete. Let us build churches that affirm rather than compare. And let us remember that in the Kingdom, victory isn't measured by applause, but by obedience and love.

PRAYER

Dear Father, in a world that measures worth by winning, help me rest in the truth that I'm already victorious through Christ. Heal any insecurity in me that strives for attention or validation through comparison. Teach me to walk in humility, honour others without envy, and find joy in their flourishing. I choose to lay down performance and pick up purpose. Let my life reflect the confidence of knowing I am accepted in the Beloved *(Ephesians 1:6 KJV)*.

In Jesus' name, Amen.

❖

CHAPTER 3

The Blame Reflex

What Led Us Here? - Where Did Things Go Wrong?

The tendency to shift blame is one of the oldest human responses to failure — and one of the most damaging to spiritual growth. We see it clearly in Genesis 3:12, when Adam, confronted by God, deflected responsibility: *"The woman You put here with me – she gave me some fruit from the tree, and I ate it"* (NIV). In a single sentence, Adam blamed both his wife and God.

WHO IS TO BLAME? *(LESSONS FROM THE FALL)*

From the very beginning, mankind has wrestled with this "blame reflex." It is not just a human flaw — it's a spiritual issue. When we blame others, we often hide our own insecurity, deflecting the discomfort of being exposed. Like Adam, we instinctively try to appear more righteous by pointing at someone else.

But blaming is not a path to healing — it is a roadblock to maturity. As long as we avoid ownership of our struggles, we will remain spiritually stunted. "If we claim to be without sin, we deceive ourselves and the truth is not in us" *(1 John 1:8 NIV)*. Growth begins with honesty.

Blame doesn't always look dramatic. It can show up subtly in daily frustrations:

- "If I had a better upbringing…"
- "If my spouse were more supportive…"
- "If my boss appreciated me…"
- "If I had more time… then I'd pray, study, and grow."

Even in ministry, we hear echoes of blame: "If I had their resources… If I pastored their church… If I had that kind of platform…" But comparison and criticism are simply insecurity in disguise.

ACCOUNTABILITY VS. ACCUSATION

The truth is: **God has given us everything we need for life and godliness** *(2 Peter 1:3 AMP)*. The question is not who is to blame — but will we take personal responsibility and walk in what Christ has made available?

Blame is a thief. It robs us of joy, accountability, and the opportunity for true transformation. Worse still, if unchecked, it can breed bitterness — even toward God. Quiet resentment whispers: "Why did You make me like this, Lord?" "Why was I born into this family, this situation, this body?"

But Isaiah 45:9 *(KJV)* reminds us soberly: *"Shall the clay say to him that fashioneth it, What makest thou?"* When we blame God, we forget that **He makes all things beautiful in His time** *(Ecclesiastes 3:11 NIV)* and that His plans for us are good *(Jeremiah 29:11 TPT)*.

Healing begins when we let go of excuses and step into the identity Christ purchased for us. We are not defined by our past or by what others did or didn't do. **We are new creations** *(2 Corinthians 5:17 AMP)*, and that means we have new responses, new choices, and a new future.

So stop rehearsing what went wrong. As Paul exhorts in Philippians 3:13-14 *(NIV)*, "Forgetting what is behind and straining toward what is ahead, I press on toward the goal…" Press forward—because your identity is no longer tied to blame, but to blessing.

CONFESSION

Thank You, Lord, that I am no longer bound by the past. I am not a victim of circumstance or people. I am more than a conqueror through Christ who loves me *(Romans 8:37 KJV)*. I refuse to blame others—I take responsibility for my growth. Your Spirit in me is greater than anything that comes against me. I will walk forward in faith, not retreat into blame. My eyes are on You.

PRAYER

Gracious Father, forgive me for the moments I've allowed blame to cover my insecurity. I surrender every excuse, every resentment—spoken or hidden. You are my Maker, and You make no mistakes. I declare today: I am fearfully and wonderfully made *(Psalm 139:14 NIV)*. Fill me with the security that comes only from You. Teach me to grow through challenges, to own my journey, and to trust that You are working all things for my good. I choose healing. I choose maturity. I choose truth. In Jesus' mighty name, Amen.

❖

CHAPTER 4

The Incapacity to Trust

Breaking the Chains of Distrust...

Insecurity often travels with a silent partner: **distrust**. Where one is found, the other usually lingers close behind. You've probably seen it—the person who won't delegate, who micromanages every detail, who wears exhaustion like a badge of honour. They may appear diligent, but beneath the surface is often a deeper issue: *they don't feel safe letting go.*

FORMED IN FEAR, REDEEMED IN CHRIST

This struggle isn't always rooted in pride—it's often rooted in fear. And fear, left unhealed, becomes the soil where distrust thrives. At its core, **distrust reveals a heart still longing to feel secure.**

Many of us grew up in homes marked by uncertainty. Whether it was financial lack, broken promises, unpredictable parents, or cultural instability, we absorbed a subtle message: *trust is dangerous.* So we learned to survive by staying guarded, staying in control. Even after coming to Christ, some believers still operate with that same internal wiring.

Our salvation changed our destiny, but for many, it hasn't yet changed their reflexes. The way we respond under pressure – whether with fear, suspicion, or control – often reveals the parts of our hearts still needing healing.

Even Jesus encountered this dynamic. As a boy of twelve, confident in His Father's calling, He was surprised when Mary and Joseph were worried about His whereabouts. "Didn't you know I had to be in My Father's house?" *(Luke 2:49 NIV)* But like many of us, they were still shaped by the instability of their time – political unrest, economic strain, and cultural fear. Distrust wasn't foreign to them; it was normal.

THE TUG OF WAR WITHIN

Israel's journey through the wilderness shows us that even after miraculous provision, insecurity can still dominate. They saw God part seas, rain manna, and guide them by fire – yet when it came time to enter the Promised Land, they shrank back. *They couldn't trust God with the next step.* Fear still ruled them.

The psalmist captures both sides of this inner battle: "When I am afraid, I will trust in You" *(Psalm 56:3 KJV)*, and later, "In God I trust and am not afraid. What can man do to me?" *(Psalm 56:11 NIV)* This is the journey we all take — from *reactive* trust to *resting* trust. From trusting God in emergencies to trusting Him in the everyday.

TRUST DELEGATED

Jesus, the most secure person to walk this earth, had no issue entrusting others. He sent His disciples to find a colt *(Luke 19:30)*, to prepare the Passover *(Luke 22:10–12)*, and even trusted Judas with the money bag *(John 12:6)*. He empowered them with Kingdom authority: "I will give you the keys of the kingdom of heaven… whatever you bind on earth will be bound in heaven" *(Matthew 16:19 NIV)*.

Delegation is not weakness — it's a fruit of trust. But many leaders, spouses, and parents struggle here. Why? Because they fear loss of control, failure, or rejection. Insecurity whispers, *If I don't do it myself, it might not get done right.* But the heart of trust says, *God is ultimately in control — even when I am not.*

A HOME BUILT ON TRUST

Distrust doesn't automatically vanish in marriage. In fact, unhealed insecurity can magnify behind closed doors. The spouse who avoids emotional vulnerability… the one who withholds affection or controls the finances — it's often not power they seek, but safety. That's why **honest conversation matters.** As James 5:16 reminds us, "Confess your faults one to another, and pray one for another, that ye may be healed" *(KJV)*.

When couples begin to talk openly about past wounds — fears of abandonment, performance-driven acceptance, or silent shame — they give God access to rebuild trust from the inside out.

Children, too, are watching. Kids raised in a home where trust is modelled — where love is not earned by perfection but offered freely — will grow up secure. But when harsh correction, sarcasm, or passive aggression dominate, children learn that trust is unsafe. And the cycle continues — unless we break it.

SECURE PEOPLE TRUST

Trusting others is risky — but trusting God is sure. If we truly believe He is our security, we can begin to loosen our grip. The more we rest in His sovereignty, the more peace fills our relationships. "Do not fear, for I am with you… I will uphold you with My righteous right hand" *(Isaiah 41:10 AMP)*. "I can do all things through Christ who gives me strength" *(Philippians 4:13 NIV)*. "Let the weak say, 'I am strong'" *(Joel 3:10 KJV)*.

If we trust Him, we'll learn to trust people again. We'll delegate without panic. We'll let others shine without resentment. We'll stop needing control to feel secure. Because Christ is enough.

LET IT BEGIN WITH YOU

Refuse to let fear be your counsellor. Refuse to let insecurity speak louder than grace. You are not what was done to you—you are who God says you are. And He says, "You are complete in Him" *(Colossians 2:10 KJV).*

CONFESSION

I confess that where I have clung to control, I have often resisted trust. But I am learning, Lord, to trust You—and because I trust You, I can trust others. I let go of perfectionism. I lay down fear. I renounce the lie that I must do everything myself. You are my security. I am no longer a slave to fear. I am a child of God *(Romans 8:15 TPT).* In Jesus, I am enough.

PRAYER

Father in Heaven, Thank You for loving me perfectly and consistently. Heal every place in me that distrust has hidden. Where I've been let down, restore my confidence—not in people, but in You. Teach me to trust again. Help me release control and walk in the freedom of faith. I want my home, my church, and my life to reflect the peace of a person fully grounded in You. I receive Your strength today. I declare, "I will trust and not be afraid" *(Isaiah 12:2 NIV).* I am safe in your Hands and I believe in the power of trust *(Isaiah 41:10).*

In Jesus' name, Amen.

❖

CHAPTER 5

Overcoming Emotional Eating

Through Identity in Christ...

E ven Jesus, in His humanity, experienced hunger. The tempter came at His weakest physical moment and said, *"If you are the Son of God, command these stones to become bread" (v.3).* But Jesus answered with something far more powerful than food: "It is written: Man shall not live on bread alone, but on every word that comes from the mouth of God" *(v.4).*

> Then Jesus was led by the Spirit into the wilderness to be tempted by the devil. After fasting forty days and forty nights, he was hungry.
>
> Matthew 4:1–2 NIV

THE ISSUE BENEATH THE APPETITE

Obesity is often less about food and more about comfort, control, or emotional safety. Many who struggle with overeating do so not out of gluttony – but out of insecurity. The plate becomes a protector. Food becomes a friend when we feel misunderstood, unloved, unseen. This is not just a physical battle – it's a spiritual one.

Often, the roots trace back to pain: a broken home, childhood trauma, rejection, or the need to feel in control of something – anything. Many have learned to medicate pain with food. For a few minutes, sweets and snacks seem to silence the ache. But the hunger always returns. Because the soul cannot be fed through the stomach. "Pleasant words are a honeycomb, sweet to the soul and healing to the bones" – Proverbs 16:24 (NIV).

God's Word is both satisfying and healing. It reaches into places food never can. And until we let Him fill those hidden places, we'll continue feeding an appetite that isn't really for bread at all. Jesus didn't need to prove anything, notice how Satan phrased the temptation: "If you are the Son of God..." The real test wasn't about food. It was about identity.

SATAN ALWAYS ATTACKS IDENTITY IN THE WILDERNESS

He tempts us to prove our worth – to reach for something to validate ourselves. But Jesus didn't have to prove He was the Son. He knew it. His security silenced the hunger. Insecurity says: "I need more to feel okay." But Christ in us says: "I have all I need in Him."

"O taste and see that the Lord is good; blessed is the one who takes refuge in Him" – Psalm 34:8 *(KJV)*. A battle for the body, but won in the Spirit. Paul understood the tension between

body and spirit. He wrote: *"I discipline my body and keep it under control, lest after preaching to others I myself should be disqualified"* — 1 Corinthians 9:27 (ESV).

This isn't about shame. It's about training. About bringing the body into alignment with what the spirit already knows: that God is enough. We don't overcome by diets alone — we overcome by feeding on truth. Declare the Word out loud. Starve the lie. Feed the truth:

> Let the weak say, "I am strong."
>
> Joel 3:10 KJV

> With His stripes, we are healed.
>
> Isaiah 53:5 KJV

> I can do all things through Christ who gives me strength.
>
> Philippians 4:13 NIV

WHEN FOOD BECOMES AN IDOL

Not all food is sinful. But when we rely on it to manage pain, escape emotions, or create a false sense of peace, it becomes an idol. It tries to take the place of the Comforter *(the Holy Spirit)*, the Healer, the Sustainer. Paul reminds us: "You are not your own; you were bought at a price. Therefore, honour God with your bodies" — 1 Corinthians 6:19–20 *(NIV)*.

The body is not in charge. It's the servant, not the master. And while this earthly body is still in process, we are learning daily to bring it under the rule of Christ. Not through condemnation — but through surrender.

CONFESSION

Lord, I confess I have sometimes looked to food for comfort instead of You. I've allowed my appetite to rule moments You wanted to heal. But now, I say: *"I shall not live by bread alone, but by every word that proceeds from the mouth of God"* *(Matthew 4:4)*.

I declare: my identity is secure in You. I will no longer turn to food when I feel empty — I will turn to You, my Bread of Life. I receive Your strength today. I am not a victim to my cravings. I am more than a conqueror through Christ who loves me *(Romans 8:37)*.

PRAYER

Father, Thank You for understanding my weakness and meeting me in it with grace. You do not shame me — you restore me. Today I surrender every unhealthy appetite and every attempt to fill what only You can satisfy. You are the One who truly sees me, loves me, and strengthens me.

Teach me to say "no" when I must, and "yes" to Your Word. Let my tongue be trained in truth. Let my cravings shift from food to faith — from sugar to Scripture. Let me taste and see that *You* are good. And let the Bread of Heaven be my daily portion. In Jesus' name, Amen.

CHAPTER 6

Spirit-Led Thinking In a Flesh-Driven World

The Carnal Brain vs. The Mind of Christ...

One of the fiercest battlegrounds in the Christian life is not found in the world around us — but within our own thoughts. Even after we are born again, there is a lingering resistance in the flesh, particularly in the area of the mind. The carnal mind — the default, un-renewed way of thinking — is not merely a nuisance. Scripture tells us plainly: *"To be carnally minded is death; but to be spiritually minded is life and peace"* *(Romans 8:6 KJV).*

THE UN-RENEWED MIND

That is not metaphorical language. Paul goes on to say, *"Because the carnal mind is enmity against God: for it is not subject to the law of God, neither indeed can be"* (Romans 8:7 KJV). The carnal mind doesn't just resist God — it opposes Him. It lives by the old patterns of self-protection, fear, pride, lust, and unbelief.

And though your spirit is born anew, the carnal brain — the part of you that housed all your old thoughts and memories — remains. It doesn't vanish at salvation; it must be *crucified daily and renewed consistently.*

THE FLESH REMEMBERS

This is why so many believers, even after years of walking with God, still struggle with intrusive thoughts, shameful memories, or carnal desires. The brain retains what the Spirit wants to release. It remembers trauma. It stores bitterness. It replays temptations. It clings to old imaginations and makes room for fear and anxiety.

The Apostle Paul knew this battle well. In Galatians 2:20, he says, *"I am crucified with Christ: nevertheless I live; yet not I, but Christ liveth in me..."* That doesn't mean his body or brain stopped functioning — it means the rule of the flesh had to bow. He lived not by the carnal brain but by the new inner life of the Spirit.

This battle plays out even in our deepest spiritual moments. In Gethsemane, Jesus Himself wrestled with the will of the flesh. Though sinless, He felt the weight of surrender. Yet His words were the turning point: *"Not My will, but Thine be done"* (Luke 22:42 KJV). The mind of Christ always chooses surrender. It doesn't argue — it yields.

THE TONGUE: A WEAPON OF WAR

The carnal mind however, tries playing the same old loops in our minds of worry, regret, and accusation, but we don't have to allow it. In fact we have every authority to intercept those loops and cut them off. As our faith doesn't just believe — it *speaks*. Paul wrote, *"I believed; therefore I have spoken" (2 Corinthians 4:13 NIV).* Romans 10:10 reminds us, *"With the heart man believeth…with the mouth confession is made..."* (KJV) Believers must believe what they believe and then speak it! John Wimber used to say, "The problem with believers, is that they don't believe what they believe."

If we allow the brain to keep replaying the past while our spirits remain silent, we give the flesh an upper hand. But when our spirit speaks — when truth is declared — the enemy is forced to retreat. The mind of Christ doesn't reason with darkness. It *casts it down*. In Egypt darkness could be felt, because darkness is all around us. Even today, darkness is perceivable by those who consider themselves unspiritual. They just know when something is creepy for example. It can be felt. But we go a step further and discern.

Then as 2 Corinthians 10:5 commands us, we're regularly meant to, "Cast down imaginations, and every high thing that exalteth itself against the knowledge of God, and bringing into captivity every thought to the obedience of Christ," which is not passive thinking — but active, verbal and Spirit-led warfare.

VOCAL COURAGE—RECLAIMING TERRITORY

We often try to reason our way through temptation, discouragement, or fear — forgetting that the enemy is a master manipulator of thought. But when we realise that even though we can't out-smart the devil we sure can out-speak him. This realisation reshapes everything:

> Let the redeemed of the Lord SAY SO, Whom He has redeemed from the hand of the adversary.
>
> Psalm 107:2 AMP

> TELL the world how he broke through and delivered you from the power of darkness and has gathered us together from all over the world.
>
> Psalm 107:2 TPT

This verse is a call to vocal courage. Those whom the Lord has rescued — those redeemed from sin, shame, fear, or bondage — are not meant to remain silent. We are invited, even commanded, to declare aloud what He has done. How God intervened and *"broke through and delivered"* and redeemed us from *"the hand of the adversary."*

This isn't just about gratitude. It's about reclaiming territory through testimony. When the redeemed speak up, darkness is pushed back. When we *say so,* we echo the victory already won on our behalf. Silence may be safe — but speech is powerful.

"They triumphed over him by the blood of the Lamb and by the word of their testimony..." — Revelation 12:11 *(NIV)* The key is to keep SAYING SO again and again because aligning our words with truth has the ability to change our lives. "Then Jesus said …you shall know the truth, and the truth shall make you free" — John 8:31–32 *(KJV)*.

Paul said, "We have the same Spirit of faith that is described in the Scriptures when it says, 'First I believed, then I spoke in faith.' So we also first believe then speak in faith." He was quoting Psalm 116:10, where David said: "I believed, therefore have I spoken: I was greatly afflicted" — Psalm 116:10 *(KJV)*. True faith is not silent. What we believe about God in our hearts must be declared openly with our mouths:

> Even when it seems I'm surrounded by many liars and my own fears, and though I'm hurting in my suffering and trauma, I still stay faithful to God and speak words of faith. So now, what can I ever give back to God to repay him for the blessings he's poured out on me? I will lift up his cup of salvation and praise him extravagantly for all that he's done for me.
>
> Psalm 116:10-13 TPT

This ties beautifully into Romans 10:10 *(AMP)*: "For with the heart a person believes [in Christ as Saviour] resulting in his justification… and with the mouth he acknowledges and confesses [his faith openly], resulting in and confirming [his] salvation."

FROM THOUGHT TO TRIUMPH
(THOUGHTS ALONE DON'T WIN BATTLES)

This truth can change our lives forever. Because while the enemy traffics in suggestion, accusation, and distortion — being subtle and ancient — there's one thing he cannot stand against: the spoken Word of God. That's how Jesus defeated him in the wilderness. Not with silent resistance — but with bold declaration: *"It is written..."* *(Matthew 4:4)* was His weapon of choice. And it must be ours, too.

We'll never win a silent war in our thoughts alone. The Word in our hearts must become the Word in our mouths. When fear whispers, we must speak up with faith. When shame rises, we must declare righteousness. When temptation comes, we must proclaim truth out loud. As Proverbs 18:21 says, *"Death and life are in the power of the tongue."* And if Satan can't steal our faith, he'll try to silence our voices instead. We must never sanction that.

King David's life offers a vivid picture of this inner war. As a youth, he ran toward Goliath not with brute force, but with bold words: "You come to me with a sword and with a spear... but I come to you in the name of the LORD of hosts..." *(1 Samuel 17:45 ESV)* His declaration brought victory.

Yet years later, David's silence got the better of him — a single glance at Bathsheba! Whereas if David had lifted up his voice in that moment and declared what was written, then things would have gone differently. Temptation gains power — when we go quiet.

The same is true today. When temptation hits, the carnal brain will argue and justify. But the mind of Christ declares truth and chooses surrender. *"Let this mind be in you, which was also in Christ Jesus"* *(Philippians 2:5 KJV)*. Speak His Word. Praise His name. Lift your voice. Victory comes not just through belief — but through declaration.

Edmund Burke—an Irish statesman and philosopher of the 18th century—is often credited with the famous line:

> *"The only thing necessary for the triumph of evil is for good men to do nothing."* And he wasn't far wrong. Add—*"or say nothing"*—and it becomes even more complete.

Scripture makes this responsibility clear: "Open your mouth for the mute, for the rights of all who are unfortunate and defenceless. Open your mouth, judge righteously, and administer justice for the afflicted and needy"—Proverbs 31:8–9 *(AMP)*. "So if you know of an opportunity to do the right thing today, yet you refrain from doing it, you're guilty of sin"—James 4:17 *(TPT)*. In other words: silence in the face of injustice—or temptation—is not neutral, it's agreement. The righteous must not be quiet. We are called to act and to *speak*.

LIVING FROM THE SPIRIT WITHIN

Here is our great assurance: Jesus does not dwell in our carnal nature *(psyche)*. He doesn't live in our old memories either. He lives in the part of us that has been redeemed—our spirit, the new creation part of us: *"If any man be in Christ, he is a new creature: old things are passed away; behold, all things are become new"* (2 Corinthians 5:17 KJV). The new wineskin *(Matthew 9:17)*.

From this inner sanctuary flows our thoughts, desires, and faith. This is why we can say with boldness, *"I have the mind of Christ"* (1 Corinthians 2:16). Our thoughts may still try to betray us. But our spirit is always loyal *(Matthew 26:41)*.

Let it lead. Let it speak. Let the Word of God in your spirit become louder than the voice of your flesh.

This is how we win the daily war of the mind: not by trying harder, but by believing deeper and speaking clearer. Declaring truth until it rewires our thinking. Confessing Christ until our minds catch up with our spirits. When we walk in the Spirit our flesh — our carnal nature — loses its grip.

CONFESSION

I have the mind of Christ. I take every thought captive and bring it into obedience. I no longer serve the flesh — I walk by the Spirit. When the enemy attacks, I speak truth. When my thoughts rebel, I declare surrender. The carnal mind no longer rules me. I live by the Word. I speak the Word. I walk in victory.

PRAYER

Father, Thank You for giving me the mind of Christ. I no longer want to live by the impulses or memories of the flesh. Help me renew my mind daily — by Your Word, through Your Spirit. Train me to speak truth when lies rise. Teach me to praise when fear whispers. Let my tongue be a sword in Your hand, and my voice a declaration of faith. I will not stay silent in battle. I will speak what You have spoken. Let peace govern my mind, and let Your Spirit lead my life.

In Jesus' name,
Amen.

❖

CHAPTER 7

Letting Go & Living Free

Finding Freedom Through Obedience & Grace...

One of the deepest, most unyielding chains that insecurity forges is unforgiveness. It wraps tightly around the soul—not always out of hatred or rage, but often from fear, wounded pride, and a sense of powerlessness. Insecure people cling to offences the way drowning men cling to driftwood. It feels like protection, but it is a prison.

INCAPACITY TO FORGIVE *(INCLUDING SELF)*

Jesus spoke boldly and often about forgiveness—not as a suggestion, but as a command. "For if ye forgive men their trespasses, your heavenly Father will also forgive you: but if ye forgive not men their trespasses, neither will your Father forgive your trespasses" *(Matthew 6:14–15 KJV)*. He didn't leave room for interpretation. Forgiveness is not optional in the Christian life. It's central. Non-negotiable. But it's also difficult.

Unforgiveness feeds on insecurity. It says, "If I let this go, I'll lose part of myself. I won't be safe. They'll win." That's the voice of fear, not faith. And yet, many believers live from that place—afraid to release others, unwilling to trust God with their pain. It's no wonder the body of Christ often walks in spiritual frustration. We are asking God to heal us while still holding onto the very thing that's making us sick.

FORGIVENESS: A TEST OF SECURITY

Jesus told Peter to forgive "seventy times seven" *(Matthew 18:22)*. Not to give him a mathematical challenge, but to teach him that forgiveness must become a lifestyle—not a special occasion. And why do some people forgive easily, while others resist for years?

Because forgiveness is easier when you're secure. It's the insecure heart that struggles most to release an offence. Pride, fear of being misunderstood, the need to be seen as "right" — these are symptoms of a deeper wound. When you know who you are in Christ, you don't need to win the argument. You don't need revenge. You're free to forgive because your identity isn't wrapped up in the offence.

Jesus was the most secure person who ever lived. He didn't inherit sin. He wasn't shaped by the wounds of a broken world. His confidence was unshakable—so much so that even in the middle of betrayal, torture, and injustice, He could pray: "Father, forgive them, for they know not what they do" *(Luke 23:34 KJV).*

How could He do that? Because He saw the joy ahead. "Looking unto Jesus... who for the joy that was set before him endured the cross" *(Hebrews 12:2 KJV).* He didn't fixate on the pain of the present—He was anchored in the promise of the future.

THE SUPERNATURAL SECURITY OF JESUS

The most secure person to ever walk this earth was our Lord Jesus. Not once do we see Him retaliating. Not once do we find Him insecure, defensive, offended, or silently stewing. Even in the face of betrayal and brutality, He remained unmoved—anchored not in applause or affirmation, but in His Father's love.

Picture Him asleep in a storm while the disciples panicked. Why? Because divine security is not circumstantial—it's rooted in trust. Picture Him washing Judas' feet, knowing full well betrayal was in motion. That is supernatural security.

When Jesus hung on the cross, His hands nailed, His body broken, His friends scattered—what came out of His mouth was not anger or self-pity, but intercession: "Father, forgive them..." *(Luke 23:34)* He didn't just preach forgiveness—He embodied it. And He calls us to do the same, not in our own strength, but in His.

WHEN WE DON'T FORGIVE

Unforgiveness is not a passive thing—it causes damage. Physical, emotional, spiritual. There have been many cases of arthritis leaving the body within hours of individuals choosing to forgive those who have defrauded him. I've known migraine sufferers healed after years — just by letting go of a grudge. Even marriages saved after months of bitterness were dismantled by a simple, heartfelt apology.

Unforgiveness isn't just a spiritual matter — it takes a toll on the body too. Countless studies, and more importantly, lived testimonies, reveal that emotional burdens often manifest physically. The Bible has always understood what doctors are only now catching up with: unforgiveness is enormously corrosive.

I've witnessed both young and old healed from joint pain and inexplicable fatigue after letting go of bitterness. One minister I knew — barely in his thirties — suffered from swelling arthritis in both hands. He finally faced the resentment he'd buried after being financially betrayed by a fellow believer. The moment he forgave, the pain lifted.

Modern medicine might call this psychosomatic. But Scripture calls it spiritual wisdom: "A heart at peace gives life to the body, but envy rots the bones" *(Proverbs 14:30 NIV)*. Unforgiveness poisons the body like slow acid. But forgiveness is not just spiritual obedience — it's healing. Sometimes our physical restoration hinges not on more prayer, but on more mercy. "Mercy always wins over judgment!" — James 2:13 *(TPT)*

> For judgment will be merciless to one who has shown no mercy; but to the one who has shown mercy, mercy triumphs victoriously over judgment.
>
> James 2:13 AMP

We might be praying for a healing, but if unforgiveness is buried in our hearts, it will resist that healing like a spiritual infection. Jesus said the man who would not forgive his fellow servant was handed over "to the tormentors" *(Matthew 18:34 KJV)*. That's what unforgiveness does. It torments you from the inside out. It starts like a soft tyranny *(ruling and oppressing us subtly);* developing into a much harsher unrelenting and unbearable tyranny.

LOOKING FORWARD, NOT BACK

Forgiveness doesn't mean pretending something didn't hurt. It means refusing to live *from* that hurt any longer. It's not the absence of justice—it's trusting God to be your Defender. It's not weakness—it's strength under the control of the Spirit. Where we can live *from* our place in His Kingdom.

Unforgiveness always looks backward. It relives conversations. Replays the wound. Rehearses the argument. But true forgiveness looks forward. It sees what's ahead— the joy of freedom, the peace of obedience, the healing of grace.

When Jesus forgave from the cross, He wasn't just showing divine mercy—He was showing divine security. He could release His enemies because He trusted His Father. Can we say the same?

A LIFE OF FORGIVENESS

Forgiveness is not a moment. It's a mindset. It's not once-and-done. It's a posture of the heart. Some wounds take time. Some offences return in memory again and again. But if you'll keep returning to the foot of the cross, you'll find grace to release again and again.

Pray for those who hurt you. Bless them. Ask God to redeem them. That prayer will soften your heart more than time ever could. "Love your enemies, bless them that curse you, do good to them that hate you, and pray for them…" *(Matthew 5:44 KJV)* When you bless them, you break the chain. Forgiveness is not letting them off the hook. It's taking yourself off the hook.

THE SECURE HEART FORGIVES

A secure person doesn't carry grudges. They don't hold people hostage for old offences. They know their worth is not in being right—it's in being redeemed. That's the life Jesus wants for you. That's the kind of freedom He died to give. He doesn't just want to forgive your sin—He wants to empower you to forgive others. Let go of the weight you've carried. Trust the God of justice. Release the past. Step into peace.

CONFESSION

I forgive, because I have been forgiven. I let go of the offence, and I receive peace. No grudge will define me. No bitterness will shape me. I am secure in Christ. Free to forgive. Free to live.

PRAYER

Lord Jesus, You forgave me when I least deserved it. You released me when I could not free myself. Now, by Your strength, I choose to do the same for others. I surrender the offence. I give You my pain. Where I have been wounded, bring healing. Where I have been angry, bring peace. Where I have held back, teach me to release.

I choose mercy. I choose obedience. I choose freedom. In Jesus' name, Amen.

❖

CHAPTER 8

From Self to Surrender

The Cross Before Me, Self Behind Me...

One of the greatest barriers to spiritual maturity is not the culture around us, nor even the trials we walk through—but the self within us. Self-preservation. Self-importance. Self-promotion. These are the hidden idols that subtly steal the throne of our hearts. Jesus called us not to self-fulfilment but to self-denial:

> Then He said to them all, "Whoever wants to be My disciple must deny themselves and take up their cross daily and follow Me."
>
> Luke 9:23 NIV

True discipleship is not about polishing self—it's about crucifying it. And this isn't a one-time act. It's a daily decision. Why? Because self hides. It hides in our prayers, our pursuits, even our acts of kindness. But wherever self remains uncrucified, insecurity will thrive.

SELF-CENTREDNESS *(THE MIRROR THAT LIES)*

Jesus told a story of two men praying in the temple – one a Pharisee, the other a tax collector:

> The Pharisee stood [ostentatiously] and began praying to himself: "God, I thank You that I am not like other people—swindlers, unjust, adulterers—or even like this tax collector. I fast twice a week; I pay tithes of all that I get." But the tax collector… would not even raise his eyes toward heaven… but was striking his chest [in humility and repentance], saying, "God, be merciful and gracious to me, the [especially wicked] sinner [that I am]!"
>
> Luke 18:11–13 AMP

Jesus shocked the crowd by saying it was the humble man who left justified before God – not the religious one who trusted in himself. Self-centredness begins early in life. A toddler clutches a toy and declares, "Mine!" – and that instinct often matures into quiet pride, subtle comparison, or defensive self-protection. We drag those habits into adulthood, into marriage, into ministry. And unless confronted, they remain deeply rooted.

NARCISSISM & THE CULTURE OF EXTREME SELF-LOVE

We can't talk about insecurity and not talk about one of the greatest plagues of our time – NARCISSISM. Our generation

76

has been sold a seductive lie: that happiness, worth, and identity come from self-love. But this isn't the love God calls us to — it's love for an image. A reflection. A curated, filtered version of "me."

This extreme form of self-love — what Scripture calls *vain conceit* — often disguises itself as confidence. But underneath is usually pain. Fear. Insecurity. It's not just pride — it's a shaky throne built on the applause of others.

> But you need to be aware that in the final days the culture of society will become extremely fierce. People will be self-centred lovers of themselves and obsessed with money. They will boast of great things as they strut around in their arrogant pride and mock all that is right. They will ignore their own families. They will be ungrateful and ungodly. They will become addicted to hateful and malicious slander.
>
> Slaves to their desires, they will be ferocious, belligerent haters of what is good and right. With brutal treachery, they will act without restraint, bigoted and wrapped in clouds of their conceit. They will find their delight in the pleasures of this world more than the pleasures of the loving God. They may pretend to have a respect for God, but in reality they want nothing to do with God's power.
>
> 2 Timothy 3:1-5 TPT

IDOLATRY *(SELF-AGGRANDISEMENT, SELF-ADORATION & SELF-WORSHIP)*

True confidence doesn't need constant attention. But narcissism feeds on it. And in a world obsessed with image — body image, platform image, sexual image — narcissism has become a form of idolatry. People aren't just promoting themselves; they're *worshipping* themselves.

Some even sexualise their own image for validation. It becomes a subtle but dangerous trap: a craving to be seen, desired, affirmed — not because they feel whole, but because they feel empty. This, too, is rooted in insecurity. It's a heart crying out, *"Am I enough?"*

But the gospel doesn't call us to adore our reflection. It calls us to die to it. "You were taught… to put off your old self, which is being corrupted by its deceitful desires… and to put on the new self, created to be like God in true righteousness and holiness" — Ephesians 4:22–24 *(NIV)*. Jesus didn't say, "Find yourself." He said, *"Lose yourself."* Not in addiction. Not in obsession. But in Him.

The most liberating thing we can do is *get over ourselves!* Because the self we're trying to prop up — through filters, affirmations, sexual approval — is not the one God redeemed. *The cross isn't meant to boost our image. It's meant to crucify it.*

"So stop fooling yourselves! If you think you are wise by this world's standards, you need to become a fool to be truly wise" — 1 Corinthians 3:18 *(NLT)*. Insecurity says, *"Look at me."* Maturity says, "How can I serve you?" We were never meant to reflect ourselves — we were created to reflect Christ.

A GENERATION BLIND TO ITS OWN EXPLOITATION (*HYPER-SEXUAL*)

We are living in a time where narcissism is celebrated and hyper-sexualisation is normalised. A generation has been deceived—exploited and exposed, yet thinking it's freedom. Modesty is mocked. Boundaries are blurred. What God designed as sacred is now performed, marketed, and consumed.

They parade their bodies, unaware they're participating in their own objectification. Culture calls it confidence, but it's often insecurity dressed up for approval. When identity is built on being wanted, the soul stays hungry for true love. This is not empowerment—it's a counterfeit. A bondage disguised as boldness. Heaven sees what the world applauds, and it grieves.

> They brag about their sins and don't even try to hide them. They are doomed! They have brought destruction upon themselves.
>
> Isaiah 3:9 TPT

THE SMALL WORLD OF THE INSECURE HEART

In general terms, insecurity is so reductive; it shrinks our worlds, till they're so tiny! Everything becomes personal—how you are seen, heard, treated. Even prayer becomes self-centred: "Lord, bless me... protect me... open doors for me..."

Of course, God invites us to bring our needs to Him. But when prayer never reaches beyond our own concerns, it reveals a heart still wrapped in self. Paul calls us to something higher: "Do nothing out of selfish ambition or vain conceit. Rather, in humility value others above yourselves"—Philippians 2:3 (NIV).

God's kingdom was never meant to revolve around "me." It's a family, a body, a bride. And where self remains on the throne, love cannot flourish.

WHEN CHURCH BECOMES ABOUT ME

Even our spiritual communities are not immune. I've watched believers pray for revival — only to bristle when it disrupts their comfort. New faces take "their" seats. Services feel unfamiliar. Yet the very change we prayed for exposes the self we never surrendered.

We can't cry out for the lost and then shut our hearts when they show up. "You shall love your neighbour as yourself [that is, unselfishly seek the best or higher good for others]" — Matthew 22:39 *(AMP)*. Real revival always breaks the mold. It widens the table. It makes room. And it demands we lay down our preferences to love people the way Christ loves us.

MARRIAGE & THE MIRROR OF SELF

Nowhere is self-centredness tested more than in marriage: "So husbands ought to love their own wives as [being in a sense] their own bodies. He who loves his own wife loves himself" — Ephesians 5:28 *(AMP)*. "Wives, be subject to your own husbands as [a service] to the Lord" — Ephesians 5:22 *(AMP)*.

Marriage exposes the residue of childhood selfishness. "My way, my time, my needs." It's not that we intend to be self-absorbed — we simply haven't surrendered that part yet.

But God calls us to something better. He calls husbands to sacrificial love. He calls wives to courageous trust. And He calls both to die to pride so that true love can grow.

Most marriage issues aren't about compatibility — they're about *self*. We want to be right more than we want to be *one*. But the remedy isn't found in your spouse changing — it's found in your heart enlarging.

WHEN RELIGION REINFORCES SELF

Even religious behaviour can mask self-idolatry. I've seen churches resist growth because "outsiders" disrupted the usual flow. I've seen long-time saints criticise the very new believers they once prayed for. We say we want the Spirit to move — but only if it doesn't move our expectations.

God is not impressed by spiritual pride. He responds to humility: "God is opposed to the proud but [continually] gives grace to the humble" — James 4:6 *(AMP)*. When we bring our insecurity to Jesus, He doesn't shame us. He transforms us.

THE PATH TO HEALING

The Pharisee spoke about himself to God. The publican simply asked for mercy. Only one left changed. We don't need more recognition. We need more surrender. The way up in the kingdom is always down. When we bow low, His grace always lifts us up. "Humble yourselves before the Lord, and He will lift you up" — James 4:10 *(NIV)*.

CONFESSION

I humble myself before You, Lord. I acknowledge the self-centredness that still lives in me. I surrender my need to be first, to be right, to be noticed. I choose to love others the way You have loved me. I will think beyond myself. I will pray beyond my comfort. I will live for something greater—Your glory.

PRAYER

My Heavenly Father, You see every place where my heart turns inward. You see the fear behind my pride, and the wound behind my need to be seen. Forgive me. I want to live surrendered—to let go of the idol of me. Teach me to love sacrificially. Let my marriage reflect Your covenant love. Let my relationships reflect Your humility. Let my life display the joy of laying my life down before you.

As you modelled this life of surrender before me, I trust You precious Lord. Help me gladly identify with your sufferings on the cross, *(Your death burial and resurrection)*. Help me keep Your cross always before me *(daily)*. And to keep myself properly surrendered. I have crossed-over. I now live from the other side of the cross. From a place that represents Your obedience and victory. Glory to His mighty name, Jesus. Amen.

❖

CHAPTER 9

Tearing Down or Building Up?

Criticism & the Spirit of Judgment...

Criticism is a subtle thief. It doesn't always sound angry or malicious — sometimes it hides behind concern, humour, or even religious conviction. But whether whispered or shouted, it can rob us of peace, poison relationships, and stunt our spiritual growth.

WHEN WORDS WOUND & THE TONGUE DIVIDES

Many of us grew up in homes where criticism was the background noise of daily life. It started with the weather and ended with the preacher. Everyone and everything was fair game for complaint — the neighbours, the teacher, the news, the church, the food, the government. Before we knew it, this lens of negativity shaped how we viewed the world — and how we spoke into it.

What begins as a cultural habit becomes a spiritual handicap. We might sing about mercy and grace on Sunday but dissect someone's choices over lunch. We say "amen" at the altar, then "ugh" at the dinner table. We wonder why our faith doesn't feel vibrant — yet we're sowing seeds of division with our speech.

> If someone believes they have a relationship with God but fails to guard his words, then his heart is drifting away and his religion is shallow and empty.
>
> James 1:26 TPT

DEATH BY A THOUSAND OPINIONS

Criticism doesn't need a microphone. It thrives in quiet corners: between friends, after meetings, in passing comments. Over time, it becomes a lens through which we see the world — a lens that always finds fault. "The tongue is a fire, a world of evil among the parts of the body... It corrupts the whole body, sets the whole course of one's life on fire…" — James 3:6 (NIV)

> The sins of your mouth multiply evil. You have a lifestyle of lies; you are devoted to deceit as you speak against others, even slandering those of your own household! All this you have done and I kept silent, so you thought that I was just like you, sanctioning evil. But now I will bring you to my courtroom and spell out clearly my charges before you.
>
> This is your last chance, my final warning. Your time is up! Turn away from all this evil, or the next time you hear from me will be when I am coming to pass judgment upon you. I will snatch you away, and no one will be there to help you escape my judgment.

The life that pleases me is a life lived in the gratitude of grace, always choosing to walk with me in what is right. This is the sacrifice I desire from you. If you do this, more of my salvation will unfold for you.

Psalm 50:19-23 TPT

Unchecked, a critical spirit becomes toxic — not only to those around us but to us. It's a false sense of superiority that slowly strangles grace and sabotages growth.

CRITICISM VS. COMPASSION
(JESUS ALWAYS CLOTHED TRUTH IN LOVE)

Jesus didn't tear people down — He lifted them up. He didn't shame — He restored. Even in correction, He clothed truth in love. Correction has a place — but it must be birthed in love, not pride. When we speak truth with gentleness, we heal. When we criticise out of insecurity, we wound:

Instead, by speaking the truth in love, we will grow to become in every respect the mature body of him who is the head, that is, Christ.

Ephesians 4:15 NIV

And never let ugly or hateful words come from your mouth, but instead let your words become beautiful [constructive] gifts that encourage others; do this by speaking words of grace to help them.

Ephesians 4:29 TPT

A HEART QUICK TO FAULT
(GRACE GIVEN IS GRACE RETURNED)

Criticism often masks insecurity. It's easier to call out flaws in others than to confront the fears within ourselves. But

85

harsh judgment? It boomerangs. And it binds us to the very standard we impose on others.

> Do not pick on people, jump on their failures, criticise their faults—unless, of course, you want the same treatment. That critical spirit has a way of boomeranging.
>
> Matthew 7:1–2 MSG

> With the measure you use, it will be measured to you.
>
> Luke 6:38 NIV

Words shape destinies — they don't evaporate. They are accumulative — good or bad — forming impenetrable layers and creating atmospheres. They shape beliefs and relationships — building and destroying — confidences.

> The tongue has the power of life and death, and those who love it will eat its fruit.
>
> Proverbs 18:21 NIV

> You must all be quick to listen, slow to speak, and slow to get angry.
>
> James 1:19 NLT

Words matter. Your mouth can be a fountain of life — or a source of destruction. The Holy Spirit desires to train our tongues: to bless, to edify, to restore. Not only in public, but also behind closed doors — around dinner tables, and in those moments of frustration.

THE DIFFERENCE BETWEEN WOUNDS THAT HEAL & ONES THAT SCAR

A secure believer doesn't need to tear others down to feel taller. You don't need sarcasm to shield your insecurity. You don't need to be the loudest to be the wisest. Compassion isn't weakness—it's maturity. "So encourage each other and build each other up, just as you are already doing"—1 Thessalonians 5:11 *(NLT)*.

Again, correction—when needed—can be laced with grace. "Faithful are the wounds of a friend [who corrects out of love and concern], but the kisses of an enemy are deceitful"—Proverbs 27:6 *(AMP)*. "It's better to be corrected openly if it stems from hidden love. You can trust a friend who wounds you with his honesty, but your enemy's pretended flattery comes from insincerity"—Proverbs 27:5-6 *(TPT)*.

We're not called to ignore sin—but we're not called to attack people either. Jesus corrected the self-righteous far more than He did the sinner. He knew when to speak—and when to weep. He knew how to restore, not just rebuke. A person of maturity knows the difference between a wound that heals and one that scars.

Bridling the tongue. If we're going to walk in the security of Christ, we must deal with our speech. Not just profanity or slander—but sarcasm, exaggeration, passive-aggression, and gossip. My general rule is this: if it doesn't help, don't do it or don't say it. This ties with Scripture: "Let everything you say be good and helpful, so that your words will be an encouragement to those who hear them"—Ephesians 4:29 *(NLT)*.

WHAT TRANSFORMATION LOOKS LIKE

It takes strength to bless when you want to blame. It takes maturity to pray when you want to point fingers. Criticism may be culturally accepted, but it is spiritually corrosive. If you want to grow deep roots in Christ, you cannot afford to carry a sharp tongue. God is calling us to be builders—not breakers. Speakers of life, not death. Every word is a seed. And what we plant today will grow tomorrow.

CONFESSION

I will not tear others down to feel built up. I will speak life, not death. I will not judge unfairly, but choose grace and truth. My tongue will be a tool for peace. My heart will stay clean from gossip and criticism. I will build others, because Christ is still building me.

PRAYER

My Father, You see every careless word I've spoken. You know where I've been quick to judge, slow to forgive, eager to speak, and reluctant to listen. Forgive me. Transform my tongue into an instrument of healing. Let my words reflect Your heart, not my insecurity. I surrender the need to be right. I choose to be righteous. Teach me to bless and not to curse, to correct in love, and to see others as You do. Let my speech be seasoned with grace. In Jesus' mighty name, Amen.

❖

CHAPTER 10

Resisting the Refiners Fire

When Pride Blocks Growth...

We all love the idea of growth. Spiritual maturity sounds noble. We want wisdom, fruitfulness, influence. But fewer of us want what actually brings it: correction.

Growth, in God's kingdom, often begins with rebuke. Not harshness or shame, but loving confrontation. It's the Refiner's fire—not punishment, but purification. Still, our flesh resists. We don't mind being encouraged, but we struggle to be corrected. We are quick to defend, slow to receive, often blind to our own blind spots.

Yet Scripture is clear: "Whoever loves discipline loves knowledge, but whoever hates correction is stupid"—Proverbs 12:1 *(NIV)*. That's not an insult; it's a warning. When we resist correction, we resist growth. We resist God.

I am the true vine, and my Father is the gardener. He cuts off every branch in me that bears no fruit, while every branch that does bear fruit he prunes so that it will be even more fruitful. You are already clean because of the word I have spoken to you. Remain in me, as I also remain in you. No branch can bear fruit by itself; it must remain in the vine. Neither can you bear fruit unless you remain in me.

I am the vine; you are the branches. If you remain in me and I in you, you will bear much fruit; apart from me you can do nothing.

John 15:1-5 NIV

A HEART THAT CAN'T BE TAUGHT

The unteachable spirit doesn't show up with banners or alarms. It hides behind spiritual language, personal preference, or emotional fragility. It says things like:

- "That's just how I am."
- "God knows my heart."
- "I already tried that."

This is not personality — it's pride. And pride, even when dressed up in Christian clothes, blocks transformation.

A wise son heeds his father's instruction, but a mocker does not respond to rebukes.

Proverbs 13:1 NIV

There is severe discipline for him who turns from the way; whoever hates reproof will die.

Proverbs 15:10 AMP

We don't outgrow correction—we grow because of it. The Holy Spirit does not merely comfort; He convicts. And one of His greatest mercies is that He confronts us, again and again, for our good.

The Apostle Paul told Timothy: "All Scripture is God-breathed and is useful for teaching, rebuking, correcting and training in righteousness"—2 Timothy 3:16 (NIV). God's Word is not just an encouragement—it's a mirror. It comforts the humble and confronts the proud. It exposes the motives we've disguised as "personality," and the stubbornness we've confused for "strength."

PRIDE IN DISGUISE

Insecurity often hides beneath pride. The most resistant people are often the most unsure inside. Correction feels like rejection because the foundation hasn't been settled: they don't truly know who they are in Christ.

That's why even children show signs of this early. A child is handed a new toy and shown how to use it—but insists on trying it their own way. Only after frustration do they return for help. Some never outgrow that response. They reach adulthood—and even faith—still unwilling to receive instruction.

I've seen it often while teaching in colleges and ministry settings. Students nod, take notes, and smile—but many listen only to critique. They're filtering every word through a lens of "Do I agree?" rather than "What is God saying to me?" That's not discernment. That's defensiveness.

Even Israel, who saw miracles firsthand, remained stiff-necked. God provided water from rocks, food from heaven, clouds by day and fire by night—and still, they would not yield. They wanted deliverance, not discipline. Presence, not purification. And they missed the fullness of what God intended for them.

It's not much different today. Many believers want blessing without refinement, influence without submission. But you cannot carry weight in the Spirit without being shaped by correction. "The Lord disciplines those he loves, as a father the son he delights in"—Proverbs 3:12 *(NIV)*. Correction is not rejection—it's proof of belonging.

THE BLIND SPOT OF THE SELF-RIGHTEOUS

Some Christians mistake stubbornness for conviction. They refuse to consider new perspectives, different teachings, or Spirit-led movements because it threatens their tradition. They say they're "standing firm in the faith"—but often, they're just afraid of being wrong.

If the Apostle Paul walked into many churches today and preached his own letters, he wouldn't be welcomed. That's not a criticism of the Church—it's a sobering reminder of how often pride insulates us from truth.

Some believers are deeply unsettled by the idea of change. They resist correction because it would mean confronting their inherited doctrines, denominational loyalties, or long-held preferences. It's easier to stay in the comfort of familiar thinking than face the discomfort of transformation. "They have refused to receive correction. They have made their faces harder than rock" — Jeremiah 5:3 *(NIV)*.

A secure believer doesn't fear truth. They aren't defensive when challenged. They know who they are in Christ — and so, they remain open, soft-hearted, and teachable.

HUMILITY IS THE POSTURE OF THE SECURE

When you know you're deeply loved by God, correction doesn't feel like condemnation. It feels like invitation. Insecure people resent others' success. Secure people learn from it. Insecure believers defend their position. Secure believers seek wisdom, even from those younger or less experienced.

Correction is not about control — it's about alignment. It's God saying, "I love you too much to let you stay where you are." "Those who disregard discipline despise themselves, but the one who heeds correction gains understanding" — Proverbs 15:32 *(NIV)*.

Humility says, "I still have room to grow." Pride says, "I already know." One leads to greater intimacy with God. The other leads to isolation — even if you're surrounded by religion.

A TEACHABLE SPIRIT CHANGES EVERYTHING

When you have a teachable spirit, you're not afraid of being wrong. You're not afraid to ask questions. You don't see correction as shameful, but as an opportunity to grow in grace. It changes how you parent, how you lead, how you receive from sermons or Scripture. You stop reading the Bible for validation—and start reading it for transformation. The proud resist correction and plateau. The humble receive it and thrive. "Humble yourselves before the Lord, and he will lift you up" —James 4:10 *(NIV)*.

PRAYER

Father, I thank You that Your correction is a sign of love—not anger. Forgive me for the times I've resisted Your voice. I confess any pride or insecurity that has made my heart hard or unteachable. Break through the walls I've built. Let Your Word soften me again. Teach me to love instruction. Shape me into someone You can trust with more. Let humility mark my walk and softness define my heart. In Jesus' name, Amen.

❖

The Final Word

The Fixer vs. The Rescuer...

Another area where insecurity can be dangerous is in the perfect example provided during the encounter between Jesus and Peter in Matthew 16:23. Notice how Jesus didn't just turn to Peter and say, "I know you're only trying to help." Instead He turned and rebuked him:

> Peter took Him aside [to speak to Him privately] and began to reprimand Him, saying, "May God forbid it! This will never happen to You." But Jesus turned and said to Peter, "Get behind Me, Satan! You are a stumbling block to Me; for you are not setting your mind on **things of God**, but on **things of man**."
> Matthew 16:22-23 AMP

Peter had good intentions. He wanted to protect the Lord, to shield Him from suffering. But his idea of care was rooted in human thinking, not spiritual revelation. It was compassion without obedience. And Jesus recognised the spirit behind it instantly—not just wrong, but satanic.

Because when human sentiment tries to shield people from the cross, it is in direct opposition to the Father's will.

NOT A COMMITTEE

This same diabolical spirit shows up again and again in apostolic ministry. It's subtle, emotional, even sincere—but it's still resistance. And I've personally encountered it often. People I love and trust offering advice, sharing concerns, trying to protect me from what they think will be too much. "Maybe don't go that far," they'll say. "You don't have to make such a strong call," or, "This could cost you influence, relationships, reputation." But the truth is, we're not called to weigh God's instruction against people's comfort. We're not running a *committee*. This is a commission—a mandate from the Spirit—and we can't fulfil it by taking counsel from *fear*.

If you're truly called—especially if you're apostolic— you must expect this kind of pressure. Well-meaning voices trying to soften what God has deliberately made sharp. Trying to delay what God has mandated as *now*. Trying to reason where God has spoken clearly. Not out of malice, but because they don't see what you see. They haven't heard what you've heard. And unless you're secure in the One who called you, you'll begin to bend—not out of wisdom, but out of insecurity disguised as empathy.

And that brings me to the other side of this same issue— because it cuts both ways. Just as others will try to rescue us from our obedience, we'll be tempted to rescue them from theirs. We'll see them at times troubled, struggling, wrestling and falling apart—everything in us will want to fix their situation or fix them! But very often, that desire doesn't come from faith. It comes from our own discomfort. From a hidden fear of failure—ours or theirs. And from a need to be the solution.

However, we are not here to be their solution or their rescuer. We are not their healer or their Saviour or their Holy Spirit. And if the Lord hasn't asked us to intervene, then our *help* becomes interference or disruption.

HUMANISM VS. SPIRITUAL PRIDE

We say it's discipleship. But if God is refining, pruning, breaking or confronting individuals—and we step in to fix them—we're just getting in His way. Trying to fix people that God is working on is not spiritual maturity—it's spiritual pride, usually because we fear how their failure might reflect on us.

Plus, fixing and rescuing people from their own cross, is not leadership—it's disobedience. Jesus didn't allow Peter to rescue Him, and neither should we. He saw through the human-sentiment and spoke straight to the source: "You're not mindful of the things of God, but of the things of MAN."

Humanism sounds spiritual, but it has no authority. It mimics compassion, while denying the power of the cross. This has infected much of the Church including modern leadership because it is a "form of godliness" that avoids anything costly. Anything sacrificial. Anything that demands obedience at the expense of approval.

But if we're going to walk in real authority, and build what God has actually called us to build, we must *break agreement with this demonic spirit.* We must reject the pressure to be understood. We must silence the voices that want to pull us down to their level of comfort. And we must be willing to walk forward — even when those closest to us want to reduce us *(to a size they're comfortable with)* or hold us back.

We must stay the course and know our mission, as Christ did His. He is supernatural in nature, a God of Miracles and Divinely powerful. He not only speaks but creates!

Your future is in His hands, Amen.
(I can see Heaven applauding.)

FORWARD OR PASS IT ON!

Note: If this book has blessed you, let it bless others. Share it, and let the message bear fruit in someone else's life. *"What you have heard... entrust to... others" (2 Timothy 2:2).* Why not sow by gifting a copy, or even placing a bundle in the hands of your home group or church? In this way the truth multiplies and glorifies our Heavenly Father.

A massive Thank You

❖

Endnotes

Bible translations

- Scripture quotations marked AMP are taken from the Amplified® Bible, Copyright © 2015 by The Lockman Foundation. Used by permission. (www.Lockman.org)

- Scripture references marked ESV are from the ESV® Bible (The Holy Bible, English Standard Version®), copyright © 2001 by Crossway, a publishing ministry of Good News Publishers. Used by permission. All rights reserved.

- Scripture references marked KJV are taken from the King James Version of the Bible.

- Scripture quotations marked MSG are taken from The Message. Copyright © 1993, 1994, 1995, 1996, 2000, 2001, 2002. Used by permission of NavPress Publishing Group.

- Scripture references marked NIV are taken from the HOLY BIBLE, NEW INTERNATIONAL VERSION ®. NIV ®. Copyright © 1973, 1978, 1984 by the International Bible Society. Used by permission of Zondervan Publishing House. All rights reserved.

- Scripture quotations marked NLT are taken from the Holy Bible, New Living Translation, copyright © 1996, 2004, 2007 by Tyndale House Foundation. Used by permission of Tyndale House Publishers, Inc., Carol Stream, Illinois 60188. All rights reserved.

- Scripture quotations marked TPT are from The Passion Translation®. Copyright © 2017, 2018 by Passion & Fire Ministries, Inc. Used by permission. All rights reserved. ThePassionTranslation.com

Drs Alan and Jennifer Pateman

are missionaries from the UK,
who at present reside in Tuscany, Italy,
and travel together as an apostolic team. They
are the Founders of Alan Pateman World Missions,
Connecting for Excellence International Fellowship,
LifeStyle International Christian University,
and APMI Publishing/Publications.

*(Please see our website for all profile and
international information, itinerant, conferences
and graduations, etc.)*

www.AlanPatemanWorldMissions.com

❖

To Contact the Author

Please email:

Alan Pateman World Missions

Email: apostledr@alanpatemanworldmissions.com
Web: www.AlanPatemanWorldMissions.com

*Please include your prayer requests
and comments when you write.*

❖

Other Books

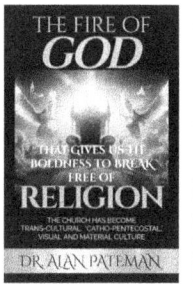

The Fire of God that Gives us
the Boldness to Break Free of Religion

This book "The Fire of God that Gives us the Boldness to Break Free of Religion" is made up of 25 Truth for Journey's that are some of Dr Alan's Letters to the Church. He points out that the Church has become transcultural, Catho-Pentecostal, visual and a material culture.

ISBN: 978-1-918102-00-0, Pages: 234,
Format: Paperback, Second Print: 2025
Also available in Hardback and eBook format!

The Python Spirit is sent to Strangle our Success

This book explores how the Python spirit operates; just as a natural python suffocates its prey, this spiritual force seeks to quench the life and authority of apostolic ministries—through financial restriction, spiritual exhaustion, and cultural resistance.

ISBN: 978-0-9570654-8-2, Pages: 218,
Format: Paperback, Published: 2025
Also available in eBook format!

ALAN PATEMAN WORLD MISSIONS.COM

Join us

in Supporting the

GOSPEL

and the work and ministry of

Alan & Jennifer Pateman

BECOME A PATRON

FOR JUST €12 A MONTH

THANK YOU
FOR YOUR CONTINUOUS SUPPORT, WE ARE FAMILY

Patrons Benefits:
1) Patrons monthly news letter
2) Personal mentoring with Dr. Alan through WhatsApp and Prayer
3) Free Book every year
4) Teaching Courses for personal study
5) Free Conference every year
6) Free Patrons Dinner   Tel: 0039 366 329 1315
         ... for those who are Hungry to be Empowered

BY DR. ALAN PATEMAN

BY DR. JENNIFER PATEMAN

AVAILABLE FROM APMI PUBLICATIONS, AMAZON.COM AND OTHER RETAIL OUTLETS

www.ingramcontent.com/pod-product-compliance
Lightning Source LLC
Chambersburg PA
CBHW071610040426
42452CB00008B/1306